The Days Between

The Days Between

Poems by

Greg Watson

© 2024 Greg Watson. All rights reserved.
This material may not be reproduced in any form, published,
reprinted, recorded, performed, broadcast,
rewritten, or redistributed without
the explicit permission of Greg Watson.
All such actions are strictly prohibited by law.

Cover design by Shay Culligan
Cover image by Kara Guelker
Author photo by Neza S.G.

ISBN: 978-1-63980-637-9

Kelsay Books
502 South 1040 East, A-119
American Fork, Utah 84003
Kelsaybooks.com

Acknowledgments

Thank you to the following publications, in which versions of these poems previously appeared:

Artistic Antidote (University of Minnesota): "Dreaming in Quarantine"
Auroras & Blossoms: "Birds Unseen," "For My Daughter"
Better Than Starbucks: "Floor Cleaner, United Hospital"
Boomer Lit Magazine: "In the MRI," "When All This Is Over"
Eunoia Review: "Following the Map of Loss," "It's Been So Long, Brother"
Little By Little, the Bird Builds Its Nest (Paris Morning Publications): "To the Treepies of Northern India"
Modern Poetry Quarterly Review: "Blue Hour," "End Page"
This Was 2020 (Ramsey County Libraries): "The Morning After"
Whistling Shade: "Things We Hardly Notice," "For My Daughter During a Pandemic"

Contents

ONE

To the Poem Not Yet Written	13
The Streets Are Deserted Now	14
A Call in the Night	15
For My Daughter During a Pandemic	16
Old Notebooks	17
Following the Map of Loss	18
The Wounded Angel	19
It's Been So Long, Brother	20
To My Double Shadow	21
The Sum of It	22
Matinee	23
Along the River	24
I Miss Losing Sleep	25
I No Longer Wait	27
Blue Hour	28
Skylight	29
To the Treepies of Northern India	30
To Drawing	32
One Star in the Sky	33

TWO

Dreaming in Quarantine	37
Birds, Again	38
Snow Shoes	39
If Indeed There Is a Body	40
Entre Nous	41
Numbers	42
On Solitude	43
To a 1969 White Fender Stratocaster	44
I Hardly Knew I Missed You	45

To Intimacy	46
To Fiction	47
Floor Cleaner, United Hospital	48
Inside	49
For My Foster Father, Edwin Anderson	50
(1928–1981)	50
Elegy for My Niece	52
Company	53
Elegy for Olli Kinkkonen (1881–1918)	54
Things We Hardly Notice	56
Speaking in Tongues	57

THREE

Birds, Unseen	61
Daylight	62
Between	63
For My Daughter	64
Finnish Tango	65
Dear Vinyl	66
Car Wash	67
Reverence	68
Coming Back to Your Body	69
All Night the Trees	70
In the MRI	71
I No Longer Look for Shapes	72
The Old Names	73
Above the City	74
Speaking Softly	75
When All This Is Over	76
End Page	77
The Morning After	78

There were days
And there were days
And there were days between
—Robert Hunter

ONE

To the Poem Not Yet Written

Eventually you will find your way,
like any wanderer left long enough in the world.
Eventually you will come knocking,
hesitantly at first, uncertain if you have
the right address; then, with a bit more force,
that calm insistence of one who has seen
much, yet has rarely been seen.
I have left many half-finished maps
scattered on floors and tabletops,
some torn, yellowing, hardly legible.
I have left the windows open for you,
birdsong punctuating the air, as if in welcome,
wing-shadow passing swift as memory.
You can talk about yourself, the way
most of us do when we speak of others,
talk about the weather, or the love
you suddenly abandoned, for reasons that
even you cannot put into words.
I, too, speak the language of bewilderment,
offering only a small measure of comfort,
and respect for the wonder of your endurance,
your steadfast allegiance to beauty
in the midst of everything saying otherwise.
My home is your home, your thoughts,
however tangled, welcomed without judgment.
Stay, dear friend, as long as you like.

The Streets Are Deserted Now

The streets are all deserted now,
the rush and congestion of their spaces
reclaimed by silence and wind.
The dusk here goes on for hours now.
Trees keep their thoughts to themselves,
hold close the laughter from summers past,
the undersides of leaves facing out.
My young daughter speaks fluently
three different languages of bird,
and the birds answer in kind.
We keep our distance from passersby,
guessing which might secretly
be witches, or animals in disguise.
The cars, like children, sleep through it all,
dreaming of faster moving days
gone by, of silver beads of rain blown
like wishes from windows and hoods.
But the streets are all deserted now,
becoming long, wayward rivers,
one turning imperceptibly into the next.
It's as if we had permission to notice,
as if all the places we thought we needed
to be were Nowhere after all.

A Call in the Night

What to make, then, of this bird calling out, long before the first glimmer of morning light? Maybe she has dreamed a human dream, I think, and woke in a terrible fright. Or maybe, like all of us, she just wanted to make sure that the world was still here. She hears the sound of her own voice echoing, one small proclamation among the silence of leaves and stars, her voice declaring only her own *bird-ness*. She feels the breeze, the air shifting imperceptibly around her song, feels the breath of something larger stirring in the dark. And she is at ease once again.

For My Daughter During a Pandemic

What will you remember of this,
my precious one, when the years have
at last collected in you like the incalculable
orbits inside the hearts of trees?

Will you recall the lengthening days
of quiet, the darkened windows of storefronts
reflecting our passing movements,
masks erasing the faces of the few others
out walking, those who, only yesterday it seems,
greeted you with smiles and waves?

Will you recall your own shrieks
of laughter playing indoors,
the elaborate forts constructed from pillows
and blankets, as if this were the safest
corner of the world we could find?

Or perhaps you will remember
the robins and house finches answering
the calls you practiced daily,
how the neighborhood rabbits became almost
unafraid—soft, gray clouds scattered
upon the lawns, allowing you to
get nearly within reach
with your outstretched hand.

I hope you will somehow remember
the wonder of the world pausing
just before it opens all at once for you.
I hope you will remember how
we still held hands while crossing
the street, though no cars
were coming from either direction;
we held each other just the same.

Old Notebooks

I have a hard time letting go of old notebooks and papers. I always think there may be something there of use years from now. They find their way from the desk to the floor, and to the kitchen table, fluttering like birds when the windows open to make themselves known. On quiet nights, I rummage through their pages, finding stray lines of poetry once familiar, half-finished thoughts, and fragments of dream. I find also quickly scribbled notes to indicate when my daughter first rolled over on her belly, or first used the toilet by herself, or the day she first reached out to me, seeking comfort through her tears. Perhaps that is what I, too, am looking for, the embrace of the familiar and true, however distant. I am reaching back, my arms open wide.

Following the Map of Loss

Cold rain tapping like a thousand leaving steps;
the rain knows the way, and it's never lost.

But the world is continually erasing us from view,
our days moving at the speed of each loss.

What can we say to the ghost gazing from the mirror?
Even our finest recollections are tinged with loss.

We mark the calendar's days as if keeping score.
Were we to lose count, there would be no loss.

Sometimes a few bad turns can lead us home.
When we love, we want nothing more than to be lost.

Every first glance contains a measure of goodbye.
When we loved, were we perfecting a kind of loss?

We learn to mourn, but for all the wrong reasons.
Without joy, we hardly remember what we have lost.

Don't believe me when I pretend to speak for the rain.
I have not yet mastered the freedom of such loss.

The Wounded Angel

from a painting by Hugo Simberg (1903)

Even the angels here must know their share of suffering, must know the very heartache peculiar to the living. Even you, passing by this moment—with bruised and bloodied wings, bandaged eyes gone dark from too much seeing, small hands that can barely hold the stem of a rose—must pass through the rubble to assist. And what of these boys who carry you now, their faces weary and resolute, their shapeless worker's clothes concealing frames not yet their own? Do they, too, know their own divinity, the sacredness of the task at hand? Their eyes say that there is no time for such thought. There is no time as you understand it. Behind you, the gray-blue of earth softens into mist, the river stretches clear and bright, innocent of thought and action. But even the angels here must know suffering, must pay their weight in flesh, to know how to measure against its opposite. They, too, must walk among the shadows of those who suffer, and those who suffer no more.

It's Been So Long, Brother

It's been so long now, brother
that I can hardly recall

which of us is the older—
you who left before age could

come to collect, or me,
the kid with a sudden shock

of white beard, eyes narrowing
even in the best of light.

Have we passed each other
without noticing, or have we

simply stepped outside
the boundaries of our years?

I speak to you now as easily
as I speak to myself,

hardly noticing the difference,
a seemingly endless string

of questions trailing off
like an old song on the radio

heard for the first time in years,
the way it faded too quickly,

the singer always cut short
before the last word could be sung.

To My Double Shadow

You tend to startle, emerging most often in winter's multiple slants of light. You prefer clean surfaces, simplicity, your steps making no discernible sound. Thin air is your home country. Yet I sense your presence enough to turn and look—and there you are, a half step behind mine, as if this were a dance I have not yet mastered. You lean back slightly upon being noticed, as if reaching for something I cannot see. Or perhaps you are just growing thin, the way we all do, returning to your secret source. We belong together only for this moment. Soon the sun will shift, the snowbanks turn their shoulders into sleep. Soon we will go our separate ways.

The Sum of It

Memory is never free.
We pay for it with experience.

Matinee

There was always a quiet understanding
between us, always the worn, unspoken comfort
of old acquaintances, just this side of laziness.
There were days when slipping inside
on chilly damp afternoons seemed both
the height of luxury and absolute necessity;
days when the world weighed too much,
and your light, however uncertain,
offered us other lives and other voices,
other loves unraveling, or somehow,
against all odds, finding the thread again.
You were always one for a good love story,
and you welcomed the rain as I did.
It seemed somehow to draw us closer.
I confess I loved it best when it was just
you and me, not another soul in sight,
the thick, musty curtains parting slowly,
seats creaking with each minor movement.
We measure too much by the body alone,
our most common misunderstanding.
You, in your unassuming way, taught us
to forget ourselves, if only for a short while,
to forget even the large, luminous faces
projected on the screen, to gaze momentarily
at that dusty circle of light, upon which
the whole flickering world depended.

Along the River

All along the river tonight,
the congregations of trees practice
their whispering songs, a few
here and there, as if carried away
by the spirit, holding a note
for as long as the wind will allow.
I listen from my own distance,
saddened that I cannot join them,
cannot offer even the smallest
praise or acknowledgement
outside of this simple refrain.

I Miss Losing Sleep

I miss losing sleep when losing sleep
meant only making love
and gentle conversation spoken
against the boundless dark.

I miss losing sleep when losing sleep
meant another bottle of red,
while the sleeping heads of trees
tossed like restless children
in the summer breeze.

I miss bargaining with poems
that refuse to lie down.

I miss having to hear that song
just one more time before calling
the city in by name.

I miss losing sleep when losing sleep
meant only that the baby needed
to be held or fed, needed to be swayed
gently, our ship docked safely
in the harbor of our home.

I miss the silence
that was ours alone,
and therefore understood.

I miss losing sleep when losing sleep
meant gazing up at stars
not yet clouded by the smoke of
buildings choking in flames,
or tear gas lingering in the streets.

I miss not missing.
I miss.
I miss.

And I miss you and me
most of all.

I No Longer Wait

I no longer await your return
the way I once did,
a younger man cursed with the patience
and persistence of a lifetime.
I no longer draw maps
in the margins
of untranslatable books,
hoping you might somehow
stumble upon them.
I no longer know the way
from there to here,
if ever I believed that I did.
Time now is a god
begging to be believed in,
my prayers forever wandering north.
So I no longer wait,
no longer sit for hours
by the window, uncoiling this
slender rope of light,
no longer come and go
down the avenues of self.
Which means, I suppose, that
I should expect you
any moment now.

Blue Hour

I still think of you
these quiet, windless mornings,
my mind too tired to chase
such thoughts away,
hours before the birdsong
and the blue light rises,
before the sound of floorboards
creaking, from rooms that
I can never quite place.
I still think of you,
as I sometimes think
of winter near summer's end,
knowing I could not live
there forever, but missing it
when it's been gone
so long.

Skylight

You cannot show me where the rest of the sky trails off, or from where it once emerged, unseen to every human eye, but of this small corner you are certain. You hold all that arises in equal measure, though only for a moment. The moment to you is all, your endless series of photographs continually in development. The clouds show their best faces to you, as if on parade. The blue sky wipes itself clean. Even the wind, I imagine, longs for your approval, though you hardly seem to notice. And all those years ago when I was young and penniless, breathing between windowless walls, you somehow managed to make yourself known, hidden above a drop ceiling the color of worn cement. I have not forgotten the divine riches you offered, that small postcard of the universe that I have kept folded in my pocket, until now.

To the Treepies of Northern India

This, then, must be the true nature of
prayer: a pure, clawing hunger

that brings you swooping down
to steal from the stone temple walls

those small, precious votive candles
burning brightly with butter fat.

With a knowing tilt of your head,
the flame gives itself up to the wind,

a motion so slight it is hardly noticed
by the devout, or those in passing.

Who could question such unwavering
devotion, bowing and returning

throughout the bright dust of daylight?
Who could dismiss the need for sustenance

as mere thievery, the insistence
of the body as anything but sacred?

We fold our hands merely to mimic
the oneness of your form,

chant for hours merely to emulate
the clarity of your song,

longing all the while to be wrapped
in the thinnest shroud of sky.

We are humble guests, forever so,
in this home you have created.

Brilliant scavenger, fire eater,
unrepentant survivor, take what you need.

The gods will not mind.
They have all the light in the world.

To Drawing

Before words could be formed on paper, before the archways and steeples of letters opened their secret structures, you were there, offering a thousand splendid doors to walk through, unnoticed from the outside world. For hours a day I could remain happily lost within you, the color of the day ours and ours alone. Those who could leave at will we loved best—wild-eyed sailors, young men on bright and tattered carpets flying away, and always an endless array of nameless birds. Only much later, drawing with words alone, did I somehow lose you. But when my little girl draws a flaming-haired troll on a mountaintop, or rainbow-colored fish swimming in the sea below, I know very well that it's you. You have not been forgotten. You have left the door open after all these years.

One Star in the Sky

"There's only one star in the sky
tonight," my little girl says, pointing up
toward a distant pinprick of light.
"I think it came out because it loves us."
"That's right," I answer in agreement—
"And just think, it remembered us
after all this time."

TWO

Dreaming in Quarantine

Even our dreams here move slowly these days, bearing the weight and stillness of the season. The dead wander through at their ease, as they always have, having less to say than they did in life, their words more weighted now. Lovers take their time, a single touch lasting for days. Animals, too, emerge, new to the city and unafraid, even in daylight hours. They do not run. This is their world, we are reminded. We are merely guests, earning our keep with meager offerings and servitude. Last night you dreamed I was a black bear, pacing back and forth, thinking, unwilling or unable to lie down and sleep. How long have I been hidden beneath this flesh? Do I remember, even, the word for love? And if I reached for you now, would you somehow recognize my face?

Birds, Again

The birds this morning, unseen,
are chattering like families on holiday,
some singing slowly, sweetly,
others punctuating the air at random
with short, clipped phrases
meant, perhaps, to startle or amuse.
Some continually interrupt,
their voices rising, falling, and rising again.
Some simply move elsewhere,
leaving small holes in the cacophony.
Some, knowing their window
to be small, wait a good long while
before making the smallest sound.
I wonder if there will ever come a time
when their stories have all been told,
when ancestors are remembered
merely through habits and movement
the young now claim as their own?
The sunlight gathers around their voices,
the sky yielding to their forms.
Their silence, when it comes at last,
will be the silence of thousands.

Snow Shoes

I like them best in the sepia-tinted photographs inside the history museum, hanging upon the wall like strange musical instruments. What would visitors from another world make of them?, I wonder. They might ponder how to tune such strings, or what ancient sport they were intended for. I have tried and failed to master them, staggering stiff-legged through a clearing of boundless white, leaving a scattering of prints no explorer could discern. Inevitably, one foot would end up facing one direction, the other pointing toward the sky, impossible to tell which way that traveler might be heading. But, of course, we all have days like that. So, I prefer them here, upon the wall, angled like benevolent weapons, their netted shadows lengthening in the fading light, traveling such lengths while the rest of the world drifts silently into sleep.

If Indeed There Is a Body

If indeed there is a body hidden
behind your own, and a body
behind mine, lumbering in shadow,
I wonder if perhaps they meet,
exchange stories or regrets,
touch without want or expectation,
or whether they have reached
an understanding we never could,
where a shout from either
is merely an exclamation of joy
or wonder, and that shroud of silence
merely the acknowledgement of
all senses agreeing at once.

Entre Nous

We've been apart now so long that
the absence itself has become
a kind of bond. It is the language
we share, the clothing worn
to our body's shape and image,
fragrance lingering beneath the skin.
It is the thing we hold closest
between us, the way we once held
our newborn through those long nights
of teething, hunger, and colic,
an entire lifetime balanced gently
between us, then as now.

Numbers

How many years, brother, since the world of our birth stamped us and walked away? How can it be the year of your death again, so soon? As your dates fade, so do my own, that dash between beginning and end the narrowest of bridges we can ever hope to cross. Your street address has likewise disappeared, along with telephone, labor union, and social security numbers, the baseball statistics you mapped out meticulously when we were kids. What good are those figures now, and what good are the weight and measurements of the body? Every number fades, every combination canceling the other, until all that remains is a circle leading back to that inscrutable, singular *You*.

On Solitude

When I said that
I needed more space,
I meant mostly
from myself. That kind
of solitude is so
hard to find.

To a 1969 White Fender Stratocaster

I never learned to hold you
the way a lover should be held,
never learned to speak your language
with fluency or understanding,
never fully grasped your nuances
or off-the-cuff eccentricities.
Young, sullen, and brash, I would never
have admitted my secret preference
for appearance over substance.
You, of course, were made of nothing
but substance, though I could
hardly be bothered to absorb it.
My touch remained close to the surface,
though your sheen and your edges
were as smooth as porcelain, bristling
with the simple divinity of purpose,
rounding back to their source.
I wish for you what I wish for all
those I never quite learned to love:
to be so now, and to know it,
to be understood and made to sing
out loud, forgetting every word,
the way I could never master, my own
voice calling from a separate room
far inside the body, one hand held flat
against the page's unchanging face.

I Hardly Knew I Missed You

I hardly knew I missed you
until there was enough
distance between us.
Now, I can no longer see you,
but feel you nightly,
rummaging through
the wind.

To Intimacy

We know you only by all the things you are not,
and look for you there impulsively:

the long, slow curves and rivers of the body,
conversations clouded by expectation and want.

So often we mistake you for physical proximity,
dream of you when distance blows through.

We dream of you while with others, wonder if
you may find us when we are most alone.

Your darker places we dare not touch,
the unspoken declarations in hospice or battle,

the hand held for hours with no thought of time,
the death rattle which can never be *unheard,*

while your lighter side slips by almost unnoticed,
the elderly woman tucking in the shirt collar

of her spouse as she passes behind him,
the laughter between siblings over a meal.

Or that familial smell of a childhood home,
all but forgotten until you had left and returned

do we find that you have been there all along,
hiding among the guest towels and dusty shelves,

in the pillowy folds of old, worn comforters
and the damp, red-mottled soil outside,

and in that tall, gnarled Elm which held you close
for so many years, never once letting you fall.

To Fiction

I lived within your pale rooms for decades, but never quite belonged there. You kept me up so many nights, telling one story after another. I never knew what to believe. Sometimes even the names you mentioned rang false, let alone the seemingly inexplicable motivations of those behind them. I gave you time. I gave you the benefit of the doubt. Sometimes you seemed to ache within your own beauty, telling a love story so pure that it could not have been otherwise. But sometimes things became confusing. So many characters walked in and out, only to return near the end of it all. Sometimes they vanished completely. I began to look for other stories, for places and things not yet named or weighted with symbolism. I began the long process of forgetting. But no one in this life forgets completely. That is another fiction. I remember our long nights together, the intimacy beyond words. If anyone asks, I will speak kindly, bending the truth only slightly. I will say that I knew you well.

Floor Cleaner, United Hospital

Your machine so cumbersome,
so intrusive, how is it that you manage
to sail past virtually unnoticed?
Head lowered, as if in reverence,
you pass by families who nervously clutch
their Styrofoam cups, watching
and not watching the silent images
splashed across the TV screens.
The low, insistent hum of your engine
is another kind of breathing here,
a pulse and motion as welcome as any.
Past the cardiac ward, past the newborns
tucked inside their caps and mittens
you glide, rounding the corners
with the grace of the well-rehearsed.
For you, the doors open without touch,
without obstruction to your path,
as the faces of those in elder care smile
their private, knowing smiles,
from the distance of a dozen lifetimes.
Soon there will be lunch served,
soon the ritual gathering of smokers
in wrinkled scrubs and hospital gowns
huddled around the loading docks.
Soon the afternoon will fold into itself.
For you, the work day continues,
for there is always one more stretch
of floor to be covered, always one more
worn surface that needs polishing,
back and forth, until it shines.

Inside

Now that you are inside
with nowhere to go,
the whole world is yours to claim.
The unseen birds still sing
the daylight into waking,
the wild imaginings of children
still startle the sleeping trees.
Small animals burrow
silently beneath your feet,
fearless in the wet-dark earth,
while the insistent metronome of
streetlights ticks on and on,
keeping time only with itself.
There is room at last to breathe,
room to dance and tumble
on any patch of grass you like.
Now that you are inside
with nowhere to go,
the whole world is yours again.
The forests and rivers have
not yet forgotten you.
Somewhere, far from here,
your own reflection looks back
from the water's edge,
your thin arms outstretched
in unquestioning affection.

For My Foster Father, Edwin Anderson (1928–1981)

I remember most the scritch of chin stubble
against my arm, the rough comfort of it,

remember standing before the shaving mirror
with you, our faces white with lather,

how I emulated your movements until
our fresh skin shown through like daylight.

I remember quiet words, plain spoken,
the depth of strength that softness contains,

remember worker's hands that held my own,
calm and unwavering, thick fingers

that folded in prayer before meals, that tied
small shoelaces into bunny ears,

and pulled me from the danger of the street,
hands that opened the cellar door

where we crouched among the potatoes
while storm winds passed overhead.

Our time together was so brief,
as all time here must be, and when you left

this earth years later without warning,
we were, inexplicably, far apart.

But I would have proudly carried you,
as you had wished, down the church steps,

bearing the casket's weight with the others,
trying my best to appear unafraid,

as the black cars idled along the curb
and the heavy bells startled the crows to flight,

would have worn my best second-hand suit
and those clumsy funeral shoes for you.

I carry you now, within these lines.
I carry you close so that others may know

that a man, however ordinary, was here,
a man passed through, and a man remains.

Elegy for My Niece

I was surprised that you came to visit
that morning in my dream, having departed
this world so suddenly only days before;
but there you were, lying peacefully outside
the plate glass window of that musty basement
apartment I had not entered in years.
Your eyes were bright and smiling, bearing
no weight or bruising from within,
no residue of the earthly sorrow which you
tried continually to numb, to bury, to exchange
for another's on the installment plan
of what became your life. You were just a kid
at that moment, as you had always been,
lounging without care in the long summer grass,
nothing but sunlight and time holding you.
Yet when I stepped slowly toward you,
you floated backward, pulled like a stage prop,
the space between us immovable, solid
as a body neither of us could see or lay claim to;
and when I reached to touch the glass,
you were already gone, carried off on waves
of all I could not know or save you from.
Dear niece, dear Ophelia, forgive my absence,
my silence, my longing to stay on this dry island
of earth—as if these long uneven roads
were my own, as if I had any idea where
any of them might eventually lead.

Company

Solitude is hard to find
these days, now that so many
have departed.
I can't go anywhere
without seeing
the ghost of someone
I once knew.

Elegy for Olli Kinkkonen (1881–1918)

The stone must speak for you now,
a statement of fact, unpleasant,
pressed hard into the earth.
It is the marker of a working man,
one who would rather not
speak in idle terms, who would
rather not draw attention
to himself unless necessary.
But, of course, you did so
simply by being, as all of those
seen as *other* eventually do.
You quietly renounced the society
that had done so to you already,
every false promise becoming
a kind of marker for your journey
back to the country left behind,
your map drawn merely by subtraction.
Your heart had already flown
when those good patriots dragged
you from your shabby room,
already flown when you smelled
the burning tar, summer heat
breathing through the trees,
the ship's rope throwing small,
bright splinters into the air.
The stone must speak for you now,
in a way that you could not,
your quiet manner as unacceptable
to them then as your language.
Do we hear you, Olli, at long last?
Do we understand silence
to mean more than mere absence?

Though words, too, have their place,
and the words staring back
offer no salve, only themselves:
"Victim of warmongers."
The stone must speak for you,
and we must learn to listen.
If it takes a thousand lifetimes,
we must learn to listen.

Things We Hardly Notice

So much we take for granted:
the slow turn of summer
sun sparking the dust into motion,
the silent, unassuming books
waiting the entire day
for one brief, distracted touch,
the tail end of a comet stirred
calmly into your coffee, then gone.
That drab painting hanging
for decades in a musty basement
before anyone notices
the small, slanted house
clinging to the edge of the landscape,
the thumbnail-sized shadow
of a family walking slowly away.

Speaking in Tongues

What wouldn't I give to be taken
by language so completely,
to chew and consume the holy word
the way the devout did at Sunday evening
service when I was still a boy?
I remember how it would begin:
the open, trembling hands reaching
skyward, toward some gilded entrance
point unseen by the rest of us.
Then, a shout which nothing could
prepare you for, a shout strong enough
to throw heads back, and fling
grown men and women to the ground.
What, then, wouldn't I offer to be
filled with the spirit until it overflowed
in a torrent of word and non-word,
every utterance a new verb
exclaiming its own holy truth?
You could have the ground I stand upon
if I could be taken by language
so forcefully and completely,
questioning and answering in cries
low and guttural, yet somehow divine,
spitting out every secret psalm
not yet written, sounds so strange
and undeniable that you would hardly
recognize the man standing before you,
stammering, unable to explain it himself
using anything but words alone.

THREE

Birds, Unseen

The birds here are so small
you would not notice
them in passing,
so unassuming that
the thinnest of shadows could
swallow them whole;
but when they sing,
when they sing
the whole world stops
to listen.

Daylight

There is no hurry today
to our movements.
We stretch our limbs with
the calm assurance
of trees in early summer,
let our shadows wander free
from room to room.
There is no touch here
that cannot linger,
no time that is not our own.
We have wandered,
it seems, for years to reach
this one bright morning.
Let the world of money
turn without us, turn until
it finds itself gone.
There is no hurry today
to our movements,
no leaving but in the wind.
Everything else moves
at the speed of daylight.

Between

What a blessing to lose
track of our days
after so long apart,
no traffic passing
and no schedules to keep.
We welcome now the ghosts
we had nearly forgotten,
invite them in for tea.
Welcome, too, the chatter
of birds, naming each object
of the world before us.
What a blessing
to be counted among
the rocks and branches,
the feathery wisps of cloud,
if only for a moment,
while the moment itself
erases itself at will.
Soon whole weeks
and months may disappear,
soon even the ground
we walk upon may become
indiscernible from sky,
and we can love outside
of time, right here where we
have always belonged.

For My Daughter

I never knew what
I was looking for
in this life. I simply
peeled away all
I did not need,
and there you were.

Finnish Tango

Come closer, my love. Place your right hand in mine, your left firmly upon my back. Gently nudge your right foot between mine, as though inching open a doorway. We may never be this close again. The rules on this floor are strict, each step measured in advance. We do not smile, do not lift our feet from the floor. We may never be this close again. Sway with me in this gently melancholy key; for it is always this way, always a bit of mourning within our movements, always a bit of longing held just below the level of the heart. Sway with me, turn and turn again. We dance through famine, dance through the wars, past our ancestors who stand faceless among the trees. Turn once more, our gaze held high, the horizon just outside that blue curtained window. We are nearly there. We may never be this close again.

Dear Vinyl

You always sounded somehow
more knowing, deeper, always spoke
in warmer tones, your character
earned through experience, those tiny
pings and pops, mysterious scuffs,
and needle-thin scratches.
Nights I thought someone was throwing
pebbles at the mirrored window,
or the house was shifting into itself,
it almost always turned out to be you,
bringing me back to the moment.
I followed your fine tracks anywhere,
with neither fear nor hesitation,
my world revolving daily at a consistent
speed of thirty-three and a third.
There was only forward momentum
for you and me, only the going,
the road leading always further in.
But forward inevitably means coming
back around again, knowing that
there is no ending that lasts, no goodbye
that can't be played once more.
Like old lovers, coming and going
throughout a lifetime, we circle back,
surprised only by being surprised,
still searching, happy to see one another
here after all these years.

Car Wash

I lasted two days at the Octopus Car Wash, the first job I ever held. It was against my better judgment, as most work was in those days. I moved at the pace of the summer clouds, steady and purposeful, polishing the leather interiors, making the chrome gleam with the length of the day before it. The others moved at a frantic pace, nervous, fidgety, smoking constantly between one vehicle and the next. Even their small talk was clipped and anxious, as if they hadn't the time or the energy to finish a thought. They spoke of cars which they could never afford if they worked ten lifetimes, and longed for them more than the calendar girls pinned to the office wall. When we broke for lunch, I knew already my time there was limited—time that had been squandered for currency, time I would have to give to another job tomorrow, and all the tomorrows to come. So I moved at the pace of the summer clouds, and I watched the sky reflected in every passing hood, so blue and so boundless that it could never be taken away.

Reverence

There are things
that even a heretic
must bow down
before:

My daughter picking
dandelions,
for one.

Coming Back to Your Body

Coming back to your body
after so long apart was like coming

back to the old country, but merely
as a tourist, unable to articulate

that peculiar sense of being home
while somehow not belonging.

I recognized monuments but not
their names, remembered landmarks

passing in and out of view,
the long and gently curving roads

which led inevitably back to
where I had started from.

I lingered in the warmth of your sun
longer than the day itself,

let the lines of every map sink
into the dark rivers below.

Coming back to your body
meant also coming back to my own,

with the language we once took
for granted slipping away,

word by word, from our tongues,
before we even noticed

the silence of unseen borders
beginning to surround us.

All Night the Trees

All night the trees
reach for one another
through the thickening dark;
all night my silence
calls out to yours
along the water's edge.

In the MRI

The room is cool, empty but for the body of the machine, lights dimmed to offer a small semblance of comfort. You lie on your back in a shabby hospital gown, a failed monk who has not yet finished stitching his robes. From somewhere you hear the sound of a bell, small yet piercing. It calls the silence closer, sending the low hum of machinery back below the surface. A calm, disembodied voice reminds you not to move. You will be instructed when to breathe, it says, and when not to. In that moment between moments, you remember learning to float as a small child, trusting the strength and cradle of the water, trusting the world to hold. Whatever happens after this is simply what happens. You breathe in slowly, hold it there at the center. You do so as many times as instructed, wait patiently to hear the bell once more. Before you know it, this will all be over. Before you know it, you'll be home.

I No Longer Look for Shapes

I no longer look for shapes
among the wind-swept clouds,
but see them with the soft familiarity
of unfinished thoughts, arising,
converging, passing slowly through.
They could be mine, after all.
They might still be of use.

The Old Names

Bring out the old names once more,
the abandoned ones broken
like the tiniest of bones,
fitted into paperweights upon the desks
of gray and faceless clerks.
Bring them from the ghostly sunken ships
out beyond the sound,
from the bottom of yellowing
legal forms, and the pockets of the dead.
Bring up the names,
one by one, whose syllables
have been clipped for efficiency,
and whose vowels were blown
like smoke rings to the shifting clouds.
Let them be sung upon the wind
that does not forget, upon the silence
that yields for this and this alone.
You can find them written
beneath the flesh of birch and pine,
lingering in dark forest moss,
rippling along the half-frozen coasts.
You can find them in the coldest of stones.
They have never been lost,
they will remind you, only waiting.
My name embracing yours.
Names not spoken for centuries
until now, here in this unclaimed land
we refer to simply as Home.

Above the City

The place where we once stood,
speaking softly, wistfully,
so many years ago,
has at last been surrendered
to the wind.
Now, at last, I can hear
you quite clearly.

Speaking Softly

You say I speak too softly, and ask me to repeat. Forgive me. I learned my speech from listening to the birch trees for hours every day. I learned my speech from ill-fitted window glass humming. I learned my speech from the silence of the printed page, the weighted Books of Moses that rose skyward with no help from me. I learned my speech in cool, musty classrooms with a number 2 pencil clenched tightly between my teeth. I learned my speech by unlearning. So when you say I speak too softly, I understand, I do. Though I cannot raise my voice in the sacred space between us. But if you lean in closely, my love, I will speak to you all that words cannot convey, and all that our small corner of heaven will allow.

When All This Is Over

When all this is over, we will know for certain that we've lived through something together. Albeit, mostly apart. We'll remember the days without names, the nights of quiet laughter and ennui, the occasional swings in mood and equilibrium. We'll remember at least some of the books read, some of the ideas that momentarily passed for wisdom. We'll recall seeing more dogs than humans on the sidewalks, stars filling the city skies on smog-free evenings. Most of all, we will remember the distance, the longing for each other when we could no longer touch. In the end, it will seem a lot like love. Let's call it that.

End Page

You remind me of home,
of winter that calls the horizon
into question for miles.
No wonder I am drawn to you,
making my way through the seemingly
endless thickets of words,
through the story someone else
has been telling all along.
It was a fine story, it was, but
you are where I belong—
here, along the shore, where words
come to a sudden end,
weary and useless
as discarded machinery.
You are the place of respite,
palace of exhalation,
wind and waves erasing
themselves to begin anew.
You are my true North,
my clearing when I was certain
that none would appear.
No wonder your landscape
folds inward, as if in prayer.
I breathe you in, breathe you out
until there is no difference
between the two.
This is all we need to say.

The Morning After

Birdsong everywhere today,
yet not a bird in sight.

Even the air seems somewhat
startled, this gray and motionless air

clouded with the residue of
last night's fires, the haze of toxins

and teargas obstructing the day
like a dirty window screen,

a day weighted with the absence
of those taken, silenced.

We are not yet done breaking each
other's hearts. Not quite.

But the birds go on singing
just the same, singing for the sake

of the song, as though the world
would end without it.

About the Author

Greg Watson's work has appeared in numerous literary reviews and anthologies, and has been nominated for Best of the Net and the Pushcart Prize. He is the author of nine collections of poetry, most recently *The Sound of Light* (Whistling Shade, 2022). He is also co-editor with Richard Broderick of the anthology *The Road by Heart: Poems of Fatherhood* (Nodin Press, 2018).

For more information, visit
www.gregwatsonpoet.com

www.ingramcontent.com/pod-product-compliance
Lightning Source LLC
Chambersburg PA
CBHW071012160426
43193CB00012B/2016